Common Core Teaching for Foundational Reading Skills

Volume One: Instructional Guidance and Single Syllable Word Lists for Effective Phonics Instruction

Mary L. Spencer

An American Reading Corps Publication

Published by

American
Reading Corps

985 East Costilla Way ✣ Centennial, Colorado 80122
americanreadingcorps@gmail.com

Cover illustration by: Saddako (ShutterStock.com)
Interior Illustrations by: Eugene Ivanov (ShutterStock.com)
American Reading Corps Logo by: FreeLogoServices.com
Expectancy Illustrations by: Mary Spencer
Print on Demand by CreateSpace.com (An Amazon Company)

Printed in the United States of America

First Edition

ISBN: 978-0-9886387-0-9

For Randy Jones, Debora Scheffel and Mary Peltier, for endlessly supporting me in my eclectic educational career.

Table of Contents

Preface

In the late nineties, I began my K-12 career as a school counselor intern in a Boston-metro K-8 school. For 18 months, I worked half time under the daily supervision of my wonderful mentor, Dr. Harriet Allen. Each day, we met with special education students in the privacy of our counseling office. Our approach to counseling included a light integration of basic tutoring in reading. With no formal training, I eagerly tried to help students improve their reading. My responses to their reading errors included statements like, "Nice try! Actually, this word is …." or "That is not quite right. Can you try again?" I really thought I was helping. Shortly after I received my M.Ed. degree in counseling from Boston University, I took a job with a national reading remediation company (Lindamood-Bell®). In just a few months, I learned the basics of how to <u>really</u> teach reading. Once I gained extensive experience working with students, I began traveling across the country to struggling schools that adopted our programs. My work included the daily training of teachers. In these projects, I was blessed with multiple opportunities to co-teach with several effective teachers. I also worked with ineffective teachers and witnessed what some educators term, "drill and kill." All in all, I learned an extraordinary amount about what is effective, and not effective, in the teaching of foundational reading skills.

After spending 6 years with the reading company, I was recruited to work for the Colorado Department of Education (CDE). There, I received extensive professional development in formal techniques of literacy coaching, and how to implement school reform models, including Response to Intervention. The state-level position was grant funded, and in 2009, funds were running out. I moved on from the CDE to take a position at one of the 18 Colorado schools of education (Jones International University) as the Director of masters-level licensure programs for teachers and principals. Here, I became immersed in the world of NCATE accreditation and the national conversation about how to overhaul and improve K-12 educator preparation programs. Across all these experiences, I learned three things about the world of teaching basic reading skills. First, research studies have taught us <u>what</u> to teach during reading instruction (i.e., content). Second, research studies have outlined the teaching techniques that should be utilized during reading instruction (i.e., pedagogy), and third, far too many teachers have received insufficient training in how to assess student literacy and teach foundational reading skills.

Today, we see a convergence of initiatives designed to dramatically impact student literacy achievement by improving educator preparation programs and teacher effectiveness in the classroom. Avenues include new state laws governing educator evaluations, alternative district preparation programs, targeted professional development, competitive federal grants, infusion of private capital into public schools, and of course, the implementation of the Common Core State Standards. These initiatives speak of great change in the K-12 arena, which may deter some from a career in teaching. Thousands may leave the K-12 classroom. But, some of these initiatives will spur the development of highly effective, engaging academic programs for our students. Increasing numbers of model schools across the country will begin to demonstrate consistent student achievement, retention of effective teachers and increased community involvement. As for you and me, these new opportunities will prompt us to challenge ourselves to become even better teachers and more astute leaders within our education communities.

When you raise student literacy, it is like a rising tide. Everything goes up: student achievement, emotional well-being and broad access to opportunities in society. Wishful thinking and hard work do not guarantee effective teaching of reading. That is what I learned from my own mistakes. I believe part of the solution to closing achievement gaps lies in school-wide adoption of targeted, ongoing professional development to support and extend teacher learning. I believe in the practice of teacher-peer mentoring programs and grade-level leadership teams who use data to drive instructional decision-making. Finally, no quality reading program can exist without high quality curricula, assessments and other resource tools designed to support both effective and accelerated instruction. The good news is that there are increasing numbers of schools of education and professional developers who have the experience needed to train pre-service and in-service educators on all components of effective literacy instruction. Additionally, numerous resource banks are now at your fingertips, most at no charge to you ("google" Center on Instruction). This book is a resource with guidance on how to effectively develop student automaticity with decoding single syllable words of varying complexity. It is the first book in a series focused on effective teaching techniques for Common Core foundational reading skills.

In close, I encourage you to seek out the resources and professional development available today to refine your instructional expertise in the teaching of foundational reading skills. As you master new levels of effectiveness, do not be surprised when others begin to solicit you to help them reach their own potential. We need to help each other, and the more of us there are, the more impact we will have. We are charged with a great responsibility to teach our kids how to read. Research says (Voice of Evidence, 2004) that, under proper instruction, only 4-6% of students will not be able to acquire basic reading skills. National reading assessments (NAEP, 2011) leave some mistakenly believing the percentage is higher. The bottom line is that most kids can learn how to read, given proper instruction, numerous practice opportunities and our own perseverance to see the job through for each and every student we teach.

I wish you well in your efforts to improve your effectiveness in teaching reading. I know I still have a lot to learn myself. With hard work, we will get there. We will succeed. And, may God speed our way!

Mary L. Spencer

Common Core State Standards For English Language Arts & Literacy - Reading Standards: Foundational Skills

At the time of this publication, 45 states have adopted the Common Core State Standards (CCSS) to use as their formal content standards for literacy and mathematics. Some states, like Colorado, will adopt the CCSS by incorporating them into an existing body of standards. Educators in these states will be expected to develop student proficiency in these standards at their assigned grade level. Student achievement of the standards will be assessed using new state assessments. A consortium of 23 states are currently working together through the Partnership for Assessment of Readiness for College and Careers (PARCC) to develop one of two national CCSS assessments. A second group of 21 states are working together through the Smarter Balanced Assessment Consortium (SBAC) to develop the second of two CCSS assessments.

Outlined below are the *Reading Standards: Foundation Skills*, organized by grade level. For access to all of the *Common Core State Standards For English Language Arts & Literacy*, please visit the official website http://www.corestandards.org. In addition, I strongly recommend you utilize the practice guide developed by the Center on Instruction, titled, *Building the Foundation: A Suggested Progression of Sub-Skills to Achieve the Reading Standards: Foundational Skills in the Common Core State Standards*. You can access the document via the web address below:
http://www.centeroninstruction.org/files/Building%20the%20Foundation%2Epdf

CCSS Excerpt: *These standards are directed toward fostering students' understanding and working knowledge of concepts of print, the alphabetic principle, and other basic conventions of the English writing system. These foundational skills are not an end in and of themselves; rather, they are necessary and important components of an effective, comprehensive reading program designed to develop proficient readers with the capacity to comprehend texts across a range of types and disciplines. Instruction should be differentiated: good readers will need much less practice with these concepts than struggling readers will. The point is to teach students what they need to learn and not what they already know—to discern when particular children or activities warrant more or less attention.*

Reading Standards: Foundational Skills (K–5) for Kindergartners

Print Concepts

Demonstrate understanding of the organization and basic features of print.
a. Follow words from left to right, top to bottom, and page-by-page.
b. Recognize that spoken words are represented in written language by specific sequences of letters.
c. Understand that words are separated by spaces in print.
d. Recognize and name all upper- and lowercase letters of the alphabet.

Phonological Awareness

Demonstrate understanding of spoken words, syllables, and sounds (phonemes).
a. Recognize and produce rhyming words.
b. Count, pronounce, blend, and segment syllables in spoken words.
c. Blend and segment onsets and rimes of single-syllable spoken words.
d. Isolate and pronounce the initial, medial vowel, and final sounds (phonemes) in three-phoneme (consonant-vowel-consonant, or CVC) words.* (This does not include CVCs ending with /l/, /r/, or /x/.)
e. Add or substitute individual sounds (phonemes) in simple, one-syllable words to make new words.

*Words, syllables, or phonemes written in /slashes/ refer to their pronunciation or phonology. Thus, /CVC/ is a word with three phonemes regardless of the number of letters in the spelling of the word.

Phonics and Word Recognition

Know and apply grade-level phonics and word analysis skills in decoding words.
a. Demonstrate basic knowledge of one-to-one letter-sound correspondences by producing the primary sound or many of the most frequent sounds for each consonant.
b. Associate the long and short sounds with common spellings (graphemes) for the five major vowels.
c. Read common high-frequency words by sight (e.g., the, of, to, you, she, my, is, are, do, does).
d. Distinguish between similarly spelled words by identifying the sounds of the letters that differ.

Fluency

Read emergent-reader texts with purpose and understanding.

Reading Standards: Foundational Skills (K–5) for 1st Graders

Print Concepts

Demonstrate understanding of the organization and basic features of print.
a. Recognize the distinguishing features of a sentence (e.g., first word, capitalization, ending punctuation).

Phonological Awareness

Demonstrate understanding of spoken words, syllables, and sounds (phonemes).
a. Distinguish long from short vowel sounds in spoken single-syllable words.
b. Orally produce single-syllable words by blending sounds (phonemes), including consonant blends.
c. Isolate and pronounce initial, medial vowel, and final sounds (phonemes) in spoken single-syllable words.
d. Segment spoken single-syllable words into their complete sequence of individual sounds (phonemes).

Phonics and Word Recognition

Know and apply grade-level phonics and word analysis skills in decoding words.
a. Know the spelling-sound correspondences for common consonant digraphs.
b. Decode regularly spelled one-syllable words.
c. Know final -e and common vowel team conventions for representing long vowel sounds.
d. Use knowledge that every syllable must have a vowel sound to determine the number of syllables in a printed word.
e. Decode two-syllable words following basic patterns by breaking the words into syllables.
f. Read words with inflectional endings.
g. Recognize and read grade-appropriate irregularly spelled words.

Fluency

Read with sufficient accuracy and fluency to support comprehension.
a. Read on-level text with purpose and understanding.
b. Read on-level text orally with accuracy, appropriate rate, and expression on successive readings.
c. Use context to confirm or self-correct word recognition and understanding, rereading as necessary.

Reading Standards: Foundational Skills (K–5) for 2nd Graders

Print Concepts

(No standards are identified in this grade level for this skill. However, the skills listed in the earlier grade levels may be applicable for this grade level when students are deficient in this area.)

Phonological Awareness

(No standards are identified in this grade level for this skill. However, the skills listed in the earlier grade levels may be applicable for this grade level when students are deficient in this area.)

Phonics and Word Recognition

Know and apply grade-level phonics and word analysis skills in decoding words.
a. Distinguish long and short vowels when reading regularly spelled one-syllable words.
b. Know spelling-sound correspondences for additional common vowel teams.
c. Decode regularly spelled two-syllable words with long vowels.
d. Decode words with common prefixes and suffixes.
e. Identify words with inconsistent but common spelling-sound correspondences.
f. Recognize and read grade-appropriate irregularly spelled words.

Reading Standards: Foundational Skills (K–5) for 2nd Graders

Fluency

Read with sufficient accuracy and fluency to support comprehension.
a. Read on-level text with purpose and understanding.
b. Read on-level text orally with accuracy, appropriate rate, and expression on successive readings.
c. Use context to confirm or self-correct word recognition and understanding, rereading as necessary.

Reading Standards: Foundational Skills (K–5) for 3rd Graders

Print Concepts

(No standards are identified in this grade level for this skill. However, the skills listed in the earlier grade levels may be applicable for this grade level when students are deficient in this area.)

Phonological Awareness

(No standards are identified in this grade level for this skill. However, the skills listed in the earlier grade levels may be applicable for this grade level when students are deficient in this area.)

Phonics and Word Recognition

Know and apply grade-level phonics and word analysis skills in decoding words.
a. Identify and know the meaning of the most common prefixes and derivational suffixes.
b. Decode words with common Latin suffixes.
c. Decode multisyllable words.
d. Read grade-appropriate irregularly spelled words.

Fluency

Read with sufficient accuracy and fluency to support comprehension.
a. Read on-level text with purpose and understanding.
b. Read on-level prose and poetry orally with accuracy, appropriate rate, and expression on successive readings
c. Use context to confirm or self-correct word recognition and understanding, rereading as necessary.

Reading Standards: Foundational Skills (K–5) for 4th Graders

Print Concepts

(No standards are identified in this grade level for this skill. However, the skills listed in the earlier grade levels may be applicable for this grade level when students are deficient in this area.)

Phonological Awareness

(No standards are identified in this grade level for this skill. However, the skills listed in the earlier grade levels may be applicable for this grade level when students are deficient in this area.)

Phonics and Word Recognition

Know and apply grade-level phonics and word analysis skills in decoding words.
a. Use combined knowledge of all letter-sound correspondences, syllabication patterns, and morphology (e.g., roots and affixes) to read accurately unfamiliar multisyllabic words in context and out of context.

Fluency

Read with sufficient accuracy and fluency to support comprehension.
a. Read on-level text with purpose and understanding.
b. Read on-level prose and poetry orally with accuracy, appropriate rate, and expression on successive readings.
c. Use context to confirm or self-correct word recognition and understanding, rereading as necessary.

Reading Standards: Foundational Skills (K–5) for 5th Graders

Print Concepts

(No standards are identified in this grade level for this skill. However, the skills listed in the earlier grade levels may be applicable for this grade level when students are deficient in this area.)

Phonological Awareness

(No standards are identified in this grade level for this skill. However, the skills listed in the earlier grade levels may be applicable for this grade level when students are deficient in this area.)

Phonics and Word Recognition

Know and apply grade-level phonics and word analysis skills in decoding words.
a. Use combined knowledge of all letter-sound correspondences, syllabication patterns, and morphology (e.g., roots and affixes) to read accurately unfamiliar multisyllabic words in context and out of context.

Fluency

Read with sufficient accuracy and fluency to support comprehension.
a. Read on-level text with purpose and understanding.
b. Read on-level prose and poetry orally with accuracy, appropriate rate, and expression on successive readings.
c. Use context to confirm or self-correct word recognition and understanding, rereading as necessary.

Teaching Whole Word Decoding and Stimulating Symbol Imagery

Introduction

The ability to decode and image words with automaticity is critical to becoming a proficient reader. The moment an individual struggles to decode a word, his/her cognitive processes used to understand the meaning of the text, is significantly compromised. We all know this and have witnessed it countless of times with our students. Effective phonics instruction includes the teaching of several components including phonological and phonemic awareness, and the systematic, explicit teaching of how to decode, encode and image words. Additionally, daily opportunities for students to practice these new skills within the context of a wide range of fiction and non-fiction books is essential for developing automaticity and fluency with text.

Within this resource, I provide techniques for how to teach and strengthen word-level skills by decoding whole words. Included are word lists carefully constructed to ensure controlled introduction and practice of words of increasing complexity. It is important to note this resource does not include guidance on how to teach phonemic awareness or segment and blend sounds in words, which are fundamental steps in the teaching of word-level skills. Many phonics programs do not include guidance on providing intensive whole-word decoding opportunities, hence the need for this resource. Finally, the content and lists within this resource are not intended to replace a high quality phonics program. This book and its content should be used to supplement your phonics instruction.

General Instructional Considerations

- When teaching, incorporate communication of learning goals, corrective feedback, peer activities, careful pacing, use of choice-contrast questioning, energy and humor.
- Keep your instructional time with word-level activities to 20-30 minutes per session.
- Provide students opportunities to reinforce new word-level skills through diverse activities (e.g., classroom learning center activities, independent or peer reading, etc.). Remember, it will take some students multiple exposures to word-level patterns to develop the neural networks needed for automaticity.
- Give students opportunities to read decodable books to practice new word-level skills in context.
- Take detailed notes about student performance during small group reading instruction. For example, note which sounds and/or orthographic patterns students struggle with.

- Use progress monitors like those created by AIMSweb or DIBELS to assess students' progress in foundational reading skills. This data will help you know when to modify, repeat or accelerate instruction.

Teaching Whole Word Decoding

Instructional guidance on how to teach single syllable, whole-word decoding skills is outlined below. Please note, the guidance is provided within the context of teaching a small group of students. However, you will find it easy to modify the sequences for one-on-one instruction.

Grouping and Materials

- Use your school's process for selecting 3-5 students to participate in the reading group.
- Provide a full, stapled copy of the word lists to each student. Remember, you can email me to request a pdf student version of the lists at no charge to you.
- Establish a teacher notebook to help you keep track of daily lessons and student progress.
- Consider having at the table: small white boards and markers for all participants, paper, pencils with good erasers, and once introduced, student sets of laminated word expectancies on index cards.

Decoding Instruction

- Make a plan for how you will progress through the session. Typically, concepts or word expectancies are introduced or reviewed first, then students take turns decoding words.
- Begin the decoding session by choosing a section of 20-30 words on a list. Date the section. Explain to students they will mark a symbol for each word he/she reads. They should not mark symbols on words their fellow students read. This will allow the student and you to review performance over time.
- Instruct students to mark a $+$ for words they read correctly, a **SC** for words they self-correct on and a $\oplus$ for words they need help with.
- Students read one word when it is his/her turn. Choose students by simply going around the table. Keep the pace fast and lively. Error correct every single error (see below for guidance).
- If the students as a group demonstrate accuracy on approximately 90% or more of the words in a given list during a given session, move to a list with more complex words and choose another 20-30 words. Likewise, if the students as a group demonstrate accuracy on approximately 50% or less of the words in a given list during a given session, move to a list with less complex words.
- During each session, make brief notes in your teacher notebook regarding sounds, orthographic patterns, etc. that need continued focus during future lessons.

Sample Dialogue

🗣 Teacher (T): O.k. everyone, thank you for getting yourselves ready for our reading group! Can you believe we have been working together for three weeks now? I am so happy for us to be able to do this work together. Today, we will be reading more words that have vowel teams. But, before we begin, I would like for all of you to take out your expectancy card for this lesson. Now….on the count of three, let's all say the poem we learned for this expectancy …1…2…3…

🗣 Students (Ss): "When two vowels go walking, the first one does the talking, he's going to say his name!"

🗣 T: Most excellent! Now, let's get straight to work. On my next count of three, I want to see everyone ready to read, with your list packet open to page 22. 1….2….3…. I love how you are all facing me, ready to work! Shauna, you may go first….and remember, if you struggle with a word, we are all going to cover the word and I am going to ask you questions that will help you read the word on your own. Let's begin…..

🗣 Shauna: "fail"
🗣 Steve: "boat"
🗣 Sammy: "stay"
🗣 Sandra: "beach"
🗣 Shauna: "sock" (student made error by saying "sock" for "soak.")

🗣 T: Let's all cover that word with our hands….Shauna, when you say "sock" what vowel letter do you see for the sound, /o/?

🗣 Shauna: (student repeats sound) /o/….um. I see an "o."

🗣 T: You're right, an "o" would say /o/! Let's look at our word and see what vowel letters we have.

🗣 Shauna: Oh. There is an "oa" in this word.

🗣 T: You're right again…Think about your "Two Vowels Go Walking" expectancy and see if you can read this word on your own. I will help you if you get stuck.

🗣 Shauna: soak!

🗣 T: You got it! Let's keep going. Your turn, Steve.

Note: Some educators may believe this approach uses too much teacher language. It is a valid observation, however, many struggling readers benefit significantly from learning how to process their own errors. Try it for several sessions with your struggling readers. With most students, you will notice they will stop guessing and become more accurate after they repeatedly experience this approach. Responding to students' responses is a powerful technique that can be used in many ways. Visit this website for more techniques: http://www.criticalthinking.org/

Stimulating Symbol Imagery

Symbol Imagery is a cognitive system believed to be responsible for our brain's ability to store symbols and patterns of symbols, including numbers and words. Neuroscientific studies conducted by Georgetown University and Yale University (among others) have identified discrete areas of the brain responsible for fluent reading. Some researchers believe that systematic decoding activities and symbol imagery exercises directly develop some of these brain areas that fluent readers employ when they read. One of our greatest technical universities in the world (the Massachusetts Institute of Technology) is now studying the effects of one reading program (i.e., Seeing Stars) that incorporates intensive whole word decoding and symbol imagery exercises. One of the goals is to study the efficacy of the approach. What is unusual is that few vendors secure opportunities to have their programs reviewed by prestigious universities. It is my opinion, that this Lindamood-Bell program is being reviewed because of the overwhelming evidence in the field that it is highly effective. Of course I recommend purchasing the Seeing Stars program and their professional development services, however, some schools may not be able to afford the program. The good news is you can implement symbol imagery exercises easily into your instruction. Please see below for sample activities.

Introduction of Symbol Imagery Concept

(a) Explain the concept in a simple way, such as, 🗣 "I am going to teach you to see letters and words in your mind's eye. This will help you learn new words for reading and spelling. Picture your first name in your head. Shelley, what letters do you see in your name? Bobby, what is the first vowel letter you see in your name? Cindy, what is the fourth letter you see in your name? Eric, what is the last letter you see in your name? When you imagine your name in your head, your brain <u>sees</u> letters!" Boys and girls, this is called 'symbol imagery.' We will do some symbol imagery exercises that will help you learn new words as well as you know your name." If needed, explain the concept or definition of "symbols."

(b) 🗣 "I am going to write some letters using just my finger on the wall. See if you can tell me what letters I am writing." Write one letter at a time, clearly and slowly, and have the students tell you what you wrote. If they make a mistake, you can say, 🗣 "If I wrote a 'p,' it would look like this (wall-write a 'p'). Now, watch me write my letter again." After you have the students guess 5-7 letters, say, 🗣 "Are there REALLY letters on this wall? No! You just saw the letters in your mind's eye!"

(c) 🗣 "Now, I want you to write letters on an imaginary screen that sits at your eye level. To find the perfect imaginary screen, put your hands over your ears and elbows in front of your nose. Model for students as you are talking. Now carefully straighten your arms keeping your hands open, like this (demonstrate). Your hands should end up at eye level. Hold your hands

11

there! This is where you will airwrite your letters and words." Explain to students their letters need to be in print form, and not be too big or small. Explain that they HAVE to watch their finger as they write the letters. Many of them will not do this. They will write the letters but look at you! Give the students a very easy word and teach them to say the letter names as they write the letters. Teach them to say the letters together. Then, ask symbol imagery questions.

Sample Symbol Imagery Exercises

(a) Students Image Words From Stimulus:

-Teacher holds up small white board with a word for 3-5 seconds

-Teacher lowers white board to remove visual of word (if students can see the word, they will not use their brain to visualize it!)

-Students airwrite word with their finger, together saying the letter names out loud

-Teacher asks 3-5 students symbol imagery questions: "Sarah, what word do you see in your mind's eye?" "Steve, how many letters do you see?" "Hugh, what is the third letter you see?" "Jose, take out the ___ & put in a ___, what word do you see now?"

(b) Students Image Words Without Stimulus:

-Teacher gives either the letters for a word or the word itself

-Letters: Students airwrite letters with their finger, together saying the letter names out loud

-Word: Students say word, then silently airwrite letters

-Teacher asks 3-5 students symbol imagery questions: "Shauna, what word do you see in your head?" "Indie, tell me the letters you see for ___." "Filipe, what letter do you see after the ___?" "Jenny, add a ___ after the ___. What word do you see now?"

(c) Integrate Symbol Imagery Exercises into Your Whole Word Decoding Activity:

-For every 1 out of every 7-9 words, the teacher prompts all students to look at the word, then cover it with their hand. Students then airwrite the word, together saying letter names out loud.

--Teacher asks each student a symbol imagery question: "Steve, what is the fourth letter you see in ___?" "Shauna, tell me what vowel letters you see." "Sammy, what letter do you see after the ___?" "Sandra, tell me the letters backwards."

Symbol imagery exercises can also be a powerful way to teach students high frequency words with irregular letter patterns (e.g., irregular words like: through, again, was and most). Students should have multiple opportunities to practice symbol imagery with the same words until they are imprinted or crystallized into the brain. Peer activities, including symbol imagery games (e.g., memory), are one way you can incorporate this in your classroom. Finally, consider integrating symbol imagery exercises into mathematics. For information about using symbol imagery in math, visit: http://www.lindamoodbell.com/programs/on-cloud-nine.Aspx.

Guidance for Error Correction

Good readers process their mistakes and correct themselves. Poor readers guess a lot and make errors, with little attempt to correct themselves. Most teachers are taught to simply give students the correct answers. For example, when students make errors, the following technique is usually employed: the teacher says, 🗣 "My turn, (teacher says word, while signaling)_____, your turn, (teacher signals as student repeats word)_____." This common technique is widely used across the country and will typically work with a (small) majority of your students. However, many of your students will continue to make the same errors, or guess, over and over and over again. The following technique teaches students to process their errors, by matching what they say to what they see. This approach is a more sophisticated technique for teaching self-correction, and it is powerful and effective with all students. The way it works is you teach your students how to correct themselves by utilizing a "respond to the response" technique (yet another good practice developed by Lindamood-Bell). When a student makes an error while reading a word in isolation, the student is prompted to look away from the stimulus word, or cover it with their hand, so they can listen to your questions as you help them process their mistake. With reading in context, the teacher reads what the student read and prompts the student to play teacher and correct the mistakes. See four examples below.

(1) Student says /back/ for "bake." (cover word) 🗣 "When you said 'back' did you make the 'a' say its name or its sound? (You can repeat what they said to help them remember) You're right, you made the 'a' say its sound! Let's look at our word again. Is this a Bossy E word? Yes! Say this vowel's name /ae/ when you say this word."

OR

🗣"When you said /back/, you made the 'a' say its sound! Look at the end of this word. What letter do you see? You're right, there's a Bossy 'E' there. Read this word again. This time, say this vowel's name (point to first vowel letter) when you say the word."

(2) Student says "and" for "the" when reading in context. 🗣 (Teacher) "I am going to read what you read. See if I match the words." Zoom into the sentence and read just the phrase or the whole sentence if it is short. Point to the words as you read so the student can listen to you read the words as they look at the words. The student will almost always catch your mistake and correct it. Then have the student reread the sentence.

OR

Cover up the word, "the" and say, 🗣 "you said 'and' here. What letters do you see for 'and' (have student give letters)? Let's look at our word and see if we match." Then, have the student reread the word, then reread the sentence.

(3) Students says "mouth" for "moth." (Cover word) 🗣 "When you say 'mouth,' what two vowel letters do you see for /ou/? You're right, an 'o-u' or an 'o-w' says /ou/. Let's look at our word and see what vowel letter we have." Then, have the student reread the word.

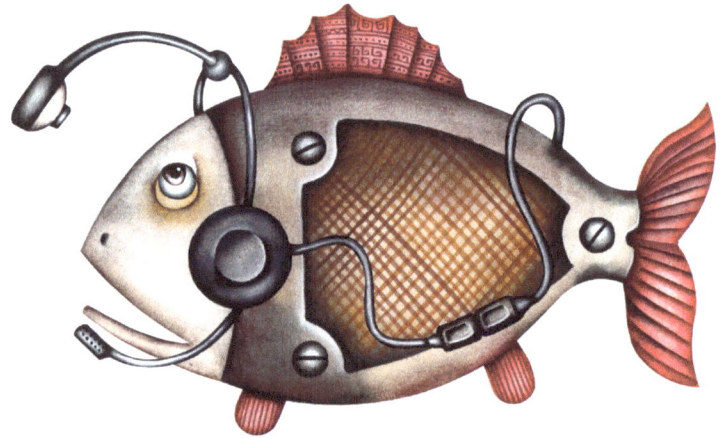

(4) Student says "bit" for "bet." 🗣 "When you say 'bit,' what letter do you see after the 'b?' You're right, it is an 'i.' We have an 'e' in this word. What does the word say now?"

(5) Articulatory feedback corrections and prompts: 🗣 "Make your mouth make these sounds." "Match your mouth to what you see." "When you said __, what was the second sound you felt your mouth making?" "When you said ___, what sound did you feel after the __?" "Use your fingers to tap out the sounds you feel your mouth making." "Feel the sounds in __. Now, spell the word."

Note: Most students do not like you interrupting them while they are reading. Consequently, they will quickly begin to self-correct on their own, without you having to go through the whole error correction dialogue, and this is o.k. Try it. You will be amazed at how quickly your students will begin to read more accurately without your assistance.

About the Word Lists

Numerous word lists are available to support reading instruction (e.g., The Reading Teacher's Book of Lists). However, few are designed for the reading intervention teacher who works with students who need controlled progression of whole word learning. The majority of struggling readers (especially those beyond the third grade) need to have daily practice opportunities in decoding and encoding to develop both a neural network to support decoding and a grade appropriate "mental word bank." Many reading lists, or choice of words, selected by teachers for phonics instruction contain words of varying complexity and regularity. The struggling reader feels most confident when he/she can apply what they know to sets of words that are regular, or in other words, "play fair." With lists containing words of varying complexity, the struggling reader becomes frustrated and often fails to develop automaticity with lower levels of words.

There will always be disagreement within the reading teacher's world about what word "rules" to teach and how to teach them. I believe the best approach is to teach students the few "rules" that work with a decent level of regularity. Also, instead of calling them "rules," call them "expectancies", "generalizations" or "tendencies" since no word rule works 100% of the time. For those instructors who may not be familiar with which word rules to employ, or who do not have a reading program, I suggest you review the six word "expectancies" outlined within this resource. These six expectancies are some of the most common "rules" or "expectancies" taught in systematic, explicit reading programs. Scripted language is presented to help you learn how to introduce the concepts.

The brain recognizes patterns and linguistic researchers (e.g., Dr. Louisa Moats) have concluded that teaching basic phonics by including a focus on orthographic patterns is the most effective approach. There are scores of good phonics programs out in the field that include orthographic activities for instruction. For example, the use of "Word Sorts" is a very popular orthographic activity known by researchers to be effective. The word lists in this book can be used with any core or supplemental program that addresses the *Foundational Skills (K-5): Phonics and Word Recognition* (PWR) standards from the *Common Core State Standards* (CCSS). Volume Two of this series will include multisyllable word lists, available in early 2013. Examples of Common Core single syllable PWR standards to be included in phonics and word recognition instruction include: common consonant digraphs, long and short vowel sounds, common word rules/expectancies (like the Final E), grade appropriate irregular words and common high frequency words. This packet includes eleven pages of word lists that were designed to directly support CCSS instruction. Instruction using the lists provides students opportunities to practice decoding words that are all regular ("they play fair") within the context of the expectancies taught. Also included, are the first two hundred words from the famous Fry Word List. The Fry list contains the most common high frequency words found in written English text. It is absolutely critical all students develop automaticity with these words. Please note the words on the Fry list include multisyllabic and irregular words. Finally, there are also three lists included that contain sentences using regular single syllable words and words from the included Fry list.

The words in the first 11 lists are leveled using the patterning system of a "C" to indicate one consonant sound and a "V" to indicate one vowel sound. Please remember that more than one letter can make up a sound. So, for example, the following three words are all CVC words: cat, shop and thick. Also, I designed the 11 lists so that words are read naturally left to right, versus up and down. Please note some of the word lists have terms that would be considered grade-level or above grade-level vocabulary terms. Teach the meanings quickly, using student-friendly definitions, but stick to the task of decoding.

Final Tips

- Use the lists as a resource for spelling/encoding words of specific orthographic patterns.

- It is o.k. to have students reread these decoding lists and you do not need to have students read words from the word lists in order. Move from list to list, as you deem appropriate.

- Countless students become confused by the language of "short" vowel sound and "long" vowel sound. Instead, use the language of "vowel sound" for the 5 short vowel sounds (a-e-i-o-u) and "vowel name" for the 5 long vowel sounds (a-e-i-o-u). This takes care of 10 out of the 18 vowel sounds! Also, the u has two long vowel "names:" /ue/ like in "use," and /oo/ like in "blue!" I was taught to call the /oo/ the u's "nickname!"

- Teach the three sounds of the -ed ending: /t/ as in "tapped," /d/ as is "plugged" and /id/ as in "traded." If a word ends in an unvoiced "quiet" sound, like /p/ as in "flip," the "ed" ending will be the unvoiced sound, /t/ as in "flipped." If a word ends in a voiced "noisy" sound, like /g/ as in "rig," the "ed" ending will be the voiced sound, /d/ as in "rigged." If a word ends in a /t/ or /d/ sound, like in "want," the "ed" ending will be /id/ as in "wanted." In "trade," the "ed" ending is also /id/ as in "traded." This /id/ ending will also add a syllable to the word. One exception to this third way of saying the "ed" ending is the word "rugged" (notice the base word ends in a /g/ sound, not a /t/ or a /d/ sound). If you do not know if a sound is "quiet" or "noisy," say the sound as you cover your ears. Quiet sounds are quiet; noisy sounds are really loud in your head!

- Remember to teach students the "n" sometimes says /ng/ like in "trunk," "sank" and "rank."

- Some students will need you to point out that the "a" sound is not always the same. Think of the "a" sound in "pat," "rat," "tack" and "map," versus the "a" sound in "Pam," "ran," "tan" and "man." Feel the difference as you say the isolated sounds of the "a" in these words.

- In this book, wherever you see letters within these symbols: / /, that is an indication to you to say the sound of the letters within the symbols, not the letter names. For example, here is an indication to say the sound of the "r:" /rrr/.

- Avoid adding an /uh/ sound at the end of consonant letters. For example, do not pronounce the sound of the "b" as "buh." Instead, isolate the sound of the "b", by producing the "b" sound quickly. You may still feel a short /uh/ sound, but it is very truncated.

- Always, always, always include "reading in text" as part of your phonics instruction! Usually, teachers have students read as the last activity. I recommend that struggling readers practice their decoding skills in text where they know 80% or more of the words. For teens, use "high-interest readers."

- Take notes about how each student is doing by jotting down unstable sounds or orthographic patterns so you know what sounds/graphemes to focus on in the next lesson (e.g., David's unstables = e, i, oi, ay, igh).

- Teach the students' parents or guardians how to practice regular and irregular words at home using simple decoding and/or symbol imagery activities.

- Participate in one of Lindamood-Bell's Seeing Stars professional development workshops, or at least, purchase the Seeing Stars manual so you can review what a comprehensive symbol imagery program looks like: http://www.lindamoodbell.com/workshops.Aspx

- Don't forget, as the purchaser of this book, you have the option to email me for a free pdf version of the 11 word lists and the 3 sentence lists at americanreadingcorps@gmail.com. Note, I will not share your email with any other entity besides my own.

Teacher Notes:

Common Word Expectancies

1. Bossy E // Silent E // Final E // Friendly E

🗣 "Words with one beat that end in 'e' are called Bossy E words. The 'e' is able to jump over one letter and make the first vowel (point to first vowel) say its name. Let's look at an example (Write 'bake' on the board). What letter do you see at the end of this word? You're right, it's an 'e' and he's Bossy! Who can tell me what this Bossy E will do in this word? You're right, he can jump over this letter and make this vowel (point to first vowel) say his name. Let me draw a silly arm to help you remember this expectancy (draw arm and thought bubble, "Say your name!"). What's the name of this letter (point to first vowel letter)? You're right, it is an 'a.' Now, say /ae/ when you say this word." **Tip:** You might have students say the vowel sound first, or have them underline the first vowel before they read the word.

Error Correction:

Student says /back/ for "bake." 🗣 (Cover word first) "When you said 'back' did you make this 'a' (point) say its name or its sound? You're right, you made it say its sound! Let's look at our word again. What do you see at the end of this word? You're right, it is a Bossy E! He's going to make this first vowel say his name. So, say this vowel's name /ae/ when you say this word."

OR

🗣"When you said /back/, you made the 'a' say its sound! Look at the end of this word. What letter do you see? You're right, there's a 'Bossy E' there. So, when you read this word again, say this vowel's name (point to first vowel letter) when you say the word."

2. D-Defender Expectancy

🗣"Some words are spelled with a -dge. The 'd' in these words protect the first vowel from the 'Bossy E.' Remember, Bossy E's cannot jump over more than one letter. We call this expectancy the D-Defender! The 'd' defends the first vowel from the 'Bossy E!' The 'Bossy E' can't make the first vowel say its name, so the vowel says its sound." Draw a picture on the board as you introduce the expectancy.

Error Correction:

Student says /bage/ for "badge." 🎤 (Cover word first) "When you said 'bage' did you make this 'a' (point) say its name or its sound? You're right, you made it say its name! You might have read it this way, because you saw an 'e' at the end of the word. Do you remember the D-Defender? Tell me about that expectancy, then let's read this word again."

3. Two Vowels Go Walking (ay - ai - oa - ea only!) Expectancy // Vowel Teams

First, draw a simple picture of a sailboat on water with a sun. Do not write the words into the picture just yet. This process of introduction makes this brief lesson more engaging.

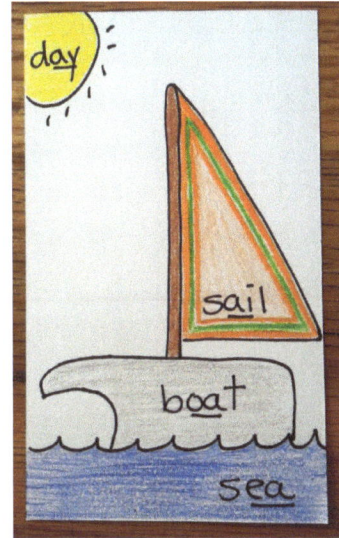

🎤"What is this a picture of? You're right it is a boat! Does anyone know how to spell the word, 'boat?'" Error handle accordingly….. Teacher writes in the word, "boat."

Continue discovering the other words as follows (variation on dialog o.k.):

🎤"What is another name for ocean?" (student(s) say, "sea.") Write word in.

🎤"What do we call this part of a boat?" (student(s) say, "sail.") Write word in.

🎤"The sun is out. Is it day or night?" (student(s) say, "day.") Write word in.

🎤"These are called vowel teams. When we see one of these vowel teams in words, they like to work together. We have a short saying that helps us remember how to say these vowel sounds. Listen. 'When 2 vowels go walking, the first one does the talking. He's going to say his name.' Point to "day." Repeat the saying as you point to the vowel letters. Ask the students, 🎤 "What's the name of this first vowel letter? You're right! It's 'a.' Now, say /ae/ when you read this word." Repeat with the other three vowel teams. **Tip:** You can either teach these 4 vowel digraphs, or "teams" for this generalization (recommended), or you can add the "ee" for a fifth digraph. Use the word "feet" or "reef" or some other single syllable word with the "ee."

Error Correction: Student says /goe - at/ for "goat." Teacher says, 🎤 (cover word first) "When you said 'goe -at,' you made the 'a' talk! Let's say our saying for vowel teams together, 'When 2 vowels go walking, the first one does the talking. He's (pointing) going to say his name.' What's the name of this first vowel? You're right, it is "o." Now, please read this word again and only say this vowel's name." **Or,** "Tell me the vowel letters you see in 'goe-at.' You're right, there is an 'o' and an 'a' in that word. The 'oa' is one of our vowel teams. Let's look at our expectancy card. You tell me what the 'oa' says. I will help you if you get stuck."

4. C-Train Expectancy

Draw a picture on the whiteboard of a train on a track that turns, with a flag (or man with lever) as pictured to the left. Have the students guess what you are drawing to keep them engaged. Draw a big "C" on the train. "What sound does the 'c' usually make? (Students say the sound, /k/......) You're right. What other letter besides the "c" makes the /k/ sound? You're right, it is a 'k.'" Write "k" many times along the track to the left of the flag. "Does anyone know the other sound the 'c' can make?" If the students do not know, give them a choice, such as: "Boys and girls, do you think the 'c' can make the /sssss/ sound or the /fffff/ sound? You're right! It can make the /sssss/ sound, like in the word, "city" (write "city" on the whiteboard). What letter besides the "c" makes the /s/ sound? ....an 's' or an 'f?'" You're right again....it is an 's.'" Once the "s" is discovered, write it many times along the track to the right of the flag. Then, introduce the expectancy. "Boys and girls, what is this a picture of? You're right, it is a train. This is the C-Train! In words, the 'c' usually says the /k/ sound. But, when it sees an 'i,' 'e,' or 'y' in a word, it will change tracks and say the /s/ sound. Let's look at some words so we can see how the C-Train will help us when we read words." Refer to the C-Train word list in this book for sample words.

Error Correction for the C-Train Expectancy: Student says /slip/ for "clip." Teacher says, (cover word first) "When you said 'slip' did you make the 'C' say the /k/ sound or the /sss/ sound? You're right, you made the 'C' say the /sss/ sound. This is a C-Train word...let's review the expectancy and see what sound the 'C' should say in this word, then you can read the word again." **Or,** "Slip is a real word! What is the first letter you see in 'slip?' ....You're right, it is an 's.' Let's look at our word to see if that matches. Then, you can read the word again."

5. G-Train Expectancy

(Draw picture first, but without letters) "Boys and girls, the G-Train is like the C-Train, but they are a little different. First, the G-Train only travels at night, but no one knows why. Sometimes, the engineers at night get sleepy and forget to change the tracks! So, when the G-Train sees a word with an 'e,' 'i,' or 'y' after the 'G' the 'G' may or may not change sounds. Here are some words where the "G" changes sounds from the /g/ to the /j/

sound: (write words on board) "gym" and "gem." And, here are some words where the "g" does not change sounds. In these words the "g" keeps saying the /g/ sound even though there is an 'e,' 'i' or 'y' letter after it: (write words on board) 'get,' 'gift,' and 'foggy.' Here's another tip, a 'g' always says the /j/ sound when it is followed by an 'e' at the end of a word like in (write words on board) 'fudge,' 'page,' 'bridge' and 'budge.' This is a goofy story, but it will help us remember how to say the two 'g' sounds in words."

Error Correction: Student says /jave/ for "gave." Teacher says, 🗣 (cover word first) "Is 'jave' a real word? You're right. It's not! Look at this word again and picture your G-Train expectancy card. Tell me first, though, what sound the 'g' will make in this word. Then, read the word again on your own." **Or,** "When you said 'jave' did you make the 'g' say the /j/ sound or the /g/ sound? You're right, you made the 'g' say the /j/ sound….This is a G-Train word…let's review the expectancy and see what sound the 'g' should say in this word. Then you can try to read the word again on you own."

6. Spelling Expectancy for TCH/CH & CK/K

Some students may benefit from learning how to spell single syllable words containing a "-tch," "-ch," "ck" and/or "k." The concept is simple and can be explained easily. 🗣 "I have a tip that will help you know how to spell words with one beat that end in a /ch/ sound. If you hear a /ch/ sound at the end of a single syllable word, think about the letters that make up the vowel sound. If one letter makes up the vowel sound, spell your word with a -tch. If two letters make up the vowel sound, spell your word with a -ch. Let's look at some words together and see how it works." Introduce the "ck"/"k" concept the same way. Below is a suggested format for how you can outline the expectancy cards.

1 Letter in Vowel Sound	2 Letters in Vowel Sound
-tch	**-ch**
patch	roach
fetch	peach
ditch	birch
botch	ouch
clutch	torch

1 Letter in Vowel Sound	2 Letters in Vowel Sound
-ck	**-k**
back	bake
peck	peek
lick	like
sock	soak
pluck	fork

General Tips:

- Some students may struggle to remember the language of the expectancy. This will not necessarily indicate they do not know how to apply the expectancy. Can they decode words that have these expectancies? That's all that really matters.

21

• Once you have introduced the expectancy, you can have the students draw their own picture of the expectancy on an index card. They can keep expectancy index cards on a ring and use them when they are in reading groups. Or, I have seen some teachers make wall posters!

• Believe it or not, these expectancies can be used with teens and adults. Just explain them in a matter-of-fact way. I sometimes say, "These are tips for young kids, and they are a bit goofy, but they sometimes help teens and adults, too."

Teacher Notes:

My Decoding Lists

Name:_____

There is no frigate like a book to take us lands away. Emily Dickinson

VC & CVC ♣ Say Vowel Sound >> a • i

1	had		2	add		3	cap		4	did		5	if	
6	nap		7	at		8	in		9	an		10	rap	
11	pit		12	sit		13	dig		14	cat		15	shag	
16	chap		17	tip		18	fan		19	fad		20	it	
21	dad		22	rat		23	zit		24	bid		25	zap	
26	bat		27	chip		28	ham		29	hat		30	hit	
31	bash		32	dab		33	sip		34	dip		35	gab	
36	it		37	sat		38	zip		39	bad		40	ship	
41	bit		42	fit		43	fat		44	gap		45	that	

Instructor Notes:	# Correct		

VC & CVC ♣ Say Vowel Sound >> e • o

1	vet		2	den		3	egg		4	shop		5	top	
6	hem		7	cob		8	dot		9	hog		10	fed	
11	odd		12	log		13	bop		14	them		15	on	
16	let		17	yes		18	hen		19	men		20	chop	
21	met		22	lot		23	fog		24	cot		25	rod	
26	not		27	cog		28	hop		29	red		30	con	
31	then		32	bet		33	Chet		34	led		35	pop	
36	Tom		37	Ben		38	mom		39	Bob		40	Ed	
41	set		42	tot		43	Don		44	fell		45	bell	

Instructor Notes:	# Correct		

+ = correct   sc = self correct   ⊕ = needed help   ♣   Students in groups only mark words they read.

CVC ♣ Say Vowel Sound >> a • e • i • o • u

1	b i t		2	c a t		3	c a p		4	d i d		5	t o p	
6	s a t		7	f a t		8	g u t		9	h o g		10	r a p	
11	f u n		12	b i d		13	d i g		14	b u g		15	s h a g	
16	g a p		17	h a t		18	f a n		19	m e n		20	c h o p	
21	m e t		22	d i p		23	c a n		24	g u m		25	s i t	
26	b a t		27	b a d		28	h a m		29	c u b		30	t i p	
31	n o t		32	h e n		33	f i b		34	h a d		35	r a t	
36	t h e n		37	f o g		38	d i m		39	n a p		40	c h i p	
41	b e t		42	h o p		43	b a s h		44	b u m		45	y e s	
46	d a d		47	c u t		48	p a n		49	l o g		50	m a t h	
51	f e d		52	l o t		53	d u g		54	c u p		55	r e d	
56	g u n		57	p i t		58	t h e m		59	s h o p		60	c h a p	
61	s u n		62	h u g		63	b u n		64	h i p		65	s a p	
66	s h i p		67	h i t		68	h u t		69	r i p		70	s u b	
71	l a p		72	g a b		73	h i m		74	h i d		75	z a p	
76	v e t		77	c o g		78	c o t		79	r u g		80	r o d	
81	h e m		82	f i n		83	f i g		84	f i t		85	s h u t	
86	C h e t		87	s h i n		88	c h u m		89	t h i s		90	t h a t	
91	b u t		92	T h a d		93	z i t		94	m a t		95	t h u d	
96	m a d		97	s h e l l		98	s h a l l		99	p a t h		100	m a p	
101	p i n		102	p e n		103	c h i n		104	t u g		105	t a p	
106	p i g		107	t h i n		108	c h u g		109	T i m		110	t a g	

Instructor Notes:	# Correct			

+ = correct   sc = self correct   ⊕ = needed help   ♣   Students in groups only mark words they read.

CVC ♣ Bossy E: Say 1st Vowel Name / Non-Final E

1	make	2	zone	3	not	4	woke	5	mile	
6	bone	7	made	8	Kate	9	tape	10	ship	
11	hike	12	back	13	net	14	note	15	time	
16	mule	17	cone	18	wake	19	puck	20	wife	
21	pick	22	hive	23	quit	24	hire	25	gate	
26	bake	27	hill	28	maze	29	fame	30	wide	
31	chill	32	rake	33	win	34	shock	35	kite	
36	Jake	37	base	38	code	39	shine	40	long	
41	rack	42	tick	43	wine	44	shade	45	pole	
46	zap	47	cute	48	case	49	hide	50	robe	
51	pile	52	sing	53	rode	54	rob	55	pill	
56	ring	57	that	58	bike	59	came	60	shop	
61	rung	62	fake	63	fire	64	this	65	pine	
66	luck	67	sack	68	lick	69	song	70	zip	
71	Rick	72	Jane	73	safe	74	hope	75	here	
76	rove	77	lung	78	tack	79	choke	80	cape	
81	rock	82	yoke	83	chop	84	pass	85	gaze	
86	those	87	shape	88	lake	89	shone	90	these	
91	Mike	92	chick	93	sham	94	Mick	95	puke	
96	sock	97	Nile	98	mole	99	shame	100	vole	
101	dive	102	date	103	dock	104	Dave	105	deck	
106	fume	107	lull	108	fuse	109	mull	110	cube	

Instructor Notes:	# Correct		

+ = correct   sc = self correct   ⊕ = needed help   ♣   Students in groups only mark words they read.

CV/CVC ✤ 2 Vowels Go Walking (2VGW) / Non - 2VGW

1	roach	2	seat	3	gear	4	rain	5	lead	
6	bead	7	coach	8	heal	9	hear	10	meal	
11	ray	12	deal	13	feat	14	tail	15	near	
16	boat	17	load	18	pail	19	neck	20	soap	
21	leaf	22	year	23	poach	24	heat	25	rack	
26	leak	27	coat	28	fear	29	sail	30	beat	
31	coal	32	may	33	tack	34	pack	35	check	
36	seal	37	rock	38	goat	39	beak	40	top	
41	rear	42	goal	43	back	44	pop	45	nail	
46	reach	47	peck	48	road	49	moat	50	loaf	
51	soak	52	match	53	gain	54	latch	55	batch	
56	sock	57	pair	58	mail	59	paid	60	main	
61	nod	62	teach	63	patch	64	veal	65	raid	
66	foam	67	fetch	68	maid	69	heck	70	peach	
71	lack	72	roam	73	hair	74	bait	75	roar	
76	rod	77	cheap	78	chair	79	say	80	day	
81	sheath	82	shun	83	chain	84	chop	85	zeal	
86	lay	87	pitch	88	wet	89	pain	90	beach	
91	leash	92	waif	93	quit	94	lain	95	bait	
96	shear	97	Cain	98	wait	99	Ned	100	Neal	
101	aid	102	toad	103	fed	104	teach	105	Heath	
106	Read!	107	red	108	sear	109	loan	110	real	

Instructor Notes:	# Correct			

+ = correct   sc = self correct   ⊕ = needed help   ✤   Students in groups only mark words they read.

↑CVC/VCC/CVCC ♣ Vowel Sounds or Names

1	act	2	write	3	end	4	ink	5	elf	
6	ding	7	dong	8	lung	9	odds	10	gang	
11	ops	12	whisk	13	wrote	14	phish	15	elk	
16	fang	17	phone	18	ask	19	ring	20	hang	
21	wing	22	knock	23	rang	24	buzz	25	elm	
26	its	27	knack	28	white	29	knife	30	whine	
31	whiz	32	whack	33	fuzz	34	rung	35	eggs	
36	fizz	37	daze	38	king	39	Kong	40	hung	
41	apt	42	fund	43	pink	44	bind	45	link	

Instructor Notes:

Remember the "n" in "nk" words = /ng/

 # Correct

↑CCVC ♣ >> oo • oo • ue • igh

1	mood	2	look	3	Sue	4	gook	5	pool	
6	flight	7	food	8	book	9	hoot	10	hoof	
11	light	12	blue	13	foot	14	due	15	loom	
16	doom	17	hood	18	boot	19	took	20	nook	
21	plight	22	noon	23	tight	24	boom	25	good	
26	stood	27	sight	28	soot	29	hue	30	shook	
31	might	32	cook	33	hoop	34	zoom	35	moon	
36	fight	37	goop	38	sigh	39	clue	40	high	
41	bright	42	true	43	cue	44	rook	45	glue	

Instructor Notes:

 # Correct

+ = correct   sc = self correct   ⊕ = needed help   ♣   Students in groups only mark words they read.

28

CCVC ♣ Say Vowel Sound

1	black		2	glass		3	plan		4	stick		5	stem	
6	clap		7	stub		8	stock		9	flock		10	trap	
11	drip		12	brick		13	fling		14	plug		15	crack	
16	grip		17	slip		18	stiff		19	sling		20	plat	
21	prod		22	clog		23	prop		24	cling		25	drum	
26	brat		27	cliff		28	bring		29	staff		30	click	
31	quack		32	Fred		33	plot		34	gloss		35	prim	
36	stuff		37	slap		38	trick		39	drop		40	flick	
41	truck		42	plum		43	quit		44	plop		45	quick	

Instructor Notes:		# Correct			

CVCC ♣ >> Say Vowel Sound

1	bats		2	dips		3	tops		4	mast		5	rocks	
6	pits		7	past		8	lids		9	rats		10	rugs	
11	wisp		12	naps		13	mint		14	shops		15	fats	
16	kids		17	risk		18	last		19	gigs		20	lint	
21	pest		22	mops		23	saps		24	rigs		25	cast	
26	locks		27	logs		28	cusp		29	rods		30	zits	
31	feds		32	disk		33	socks		34	zest		35	vats	
36	pups		37	pats		38	nods		39	cats		40	pigs	
41	odds		42	eggs		43	adds		44	apps		45	dusk	

Instructor Notes:		# Correct			

+ = correct   sc = self correct   ⊕ = needed help   ♣   Students in groups only mark words they read.

CCVCC ♣ Say Vowel Sound >> a • e • i • o • u

1	blast	2	props	3	flips	4	swept	5	stops	
6	crops	7	cramp	8	drips	9	grunt	10	stings	
11	drops	12	blocks	13	grant	14	stench	15	clips	
16	plans	17	flops	18	bricks	19	claps	20	drink	
21	stint	22	brings	23	stink	24	blimp	25	grills	
26	thrills	27	clings	28	flings	29	grump	30	prance	
31	gland	32	stunt	33	blunt	34	stand	35	trunk	
36	tricks	37	flocks	38	sticks	39	specks	40	flicks	
41	Grinch	42	steps	43	clench	44	drench	45	spots	
46	blobs	47	crimp	48	draft	49	flaps	50	plats	
51	plugs	52	dripped	53	preps	54	stats	55	slips	
56	bluffs	57	blanch	58	brisk	59	drunk	60	trench	
61	branch	62	stance	63	crabs	64	globs	65	stabs	
66	stopped	67	stepped	68	stump	69	brunt	70	flinch	
71	staffs	72	blocked	73	brunch	74	cracks	75	brats	
76	clocked	77	tricked	78	flocked	79	cliffs	80	crust	
81	clench	82	tracked	83	flicked	84	stags	85	brand	
86	prods	87	dropped	88	clunk	89	clinch	90	prince	
91	stunk	92	crept	93	stuffs	94	bland	95	flunk	
96	crunch	97	French	98	frond	99	grand	100	slept	
101	stems	102	plots	103	trucks	104	treks	105	tracks	
106	drops	107	flask	108	trips	109	flank	110	trust	

Instructor Notes:		# Correct			

+ = correct   sc = self correct   ⊕ = needed help   ♣   Students in groups only mark words they read.

↑CCVC/CVCC ♣ oi/oy • ou/ow • aw

1	towns	2	moist	3	lawn	4	dawn	5	drawn	
6	coin	7	coy	8	now	9	how	10	sound	
11	blouse	12	pouch	13	foil	14	Ouch!	15	chows	
16	boys	17	mound	18	ploy	19	cloud	20	couch	
21	mouth	22	plows	23	hoist	24	coil	25	awl	
26	round	27	south	28	house	29	Troy	30	paw	
31	cow	32	saw	33	loud	34	flaws	35	pound	
36	shout	37	jaws	38	laws	39	joust	40	Wow!	
41	choice	42	shawl	43	mouse	44	lawn	45	thaws	

Instructor Notes:	# Correct			

↑CCVCC ♣ qu • x • y >> Beware! Vocabulary Alert↓

1	quit	2	six	3	try	4	ox	5	yes	
6	yeast	7	quick	8	yep	9	my	10	quaint	
11	hoax	12	yard	13	by	14	quake	15	yoke	
16	quilt	17	shy	18	quiz	19	mix	20	quit	
21	yelp	22	jinx	23	yawn	24	quill	25	coax	
26	lax	27	quail	28	tax	29	yak	30	quip	
31	yawp	32	yell	33	quest	34	flux	35	max	
36	quack	37	x	38	flex	39	yowl	40	quell	
41	Sox	42	yurt	43	tux	44	yarn	45	flax	

Instructor Notes:	# Correct			

+ = correct   sc = self correct   ⊕ = needed help   ♣   Students in groups only mark words they read.

↑CCVC/CVCC ♣ er • ir • ur • or • ar

1	burn		2	torn		3	yarn		4	born		5	ark	
6	farm		7	birch		8	torch		9	start		10	thirst	
11	card		12	curl		13	arch		14	snarl		15	stars	
16	bark		17	turn		18	herd		19	fork		20	shark	
21	stark		22	turf		23	burst		24	hard		25	third	
26	darn		27	stirs		28	swirl		29	bird		30	yard	
31	skirt		32	horn		33	shirt		34	hurt		35	arm	
36	corn		37	dirt		38	urn		39	barn		40	churn	
41	berg		42	stern		43	Kirk		44	irk		45	cord	

Instructor Notes:	# Correct			

↑CCVCC ♣ er • ir • ur • or • ar

1	sparks		2	quirk		3	storms		4	first		5	charge	
6	chirps		7	terse		8	force		9	church		10	horse	
11	flirt		12	burns		13	purse		14	per		15	farce	
16	curse		17	cords		18	swirls		19	turns		20	squirts	
21	parse		22	churns		23	sparse		24	nor		25	blur	
26	charms		27	spar		28	swerve		29	char		30	verse	
31	sirs		32	herds		33	slur		34	shirk		35	charts	
36	carts		37	char		38	scars		39	snarls		40	nurse	
41	nerve		42	serve		43	sharp		44	carve		45	curve	

Instructor Notes:	# Correct			

+ = correct   sc = self correct   ⊕ = needed help   ♣ Students in groups only mark words they read.

↑CCVCC ♣ C - Train >> Vowel Names and Sounds

1	clown	2	pace	3	lice	4	choice	5	cork
6	cell	7	cease	8	crimp	9	cod	10	crabs
11	lace	12	cite	13	disc	14	ice	15	mince
16	Vince	17	place	18	clicks	19	cots	20	camp
21	cinch	22	clip	23	cam	24	cramp	25	clock
26	mice	27	cast	28	crack	29	sauce	30	cusp
31	cyst	32	cots	33	trace	34	cog	35	voice
36	claim	37	rice	38	grace	39	clams	40	cent
41	clans	42	farce	43	clinch	44	Bruce	45	talc

Instructor Notes:	# Correct		

↑CCVCC ♣ G-Train >> Vowel Names and Sounds

1	page	2	gate	3	rage	4	green	5	fudge
6	fridge	7	globs	8	gouge	9	goof	10	grain
11	huge	12	drug	13	hugs	14	gap	15	mug
16	sage	17	budge	18	glad	19	goop	20	ridge
21	grab	22	surge	23	gown	24	bugs	25	tags
26	gain	27	pegs	28	plugs	29	lodge	30	nudge
31	wedge	32	edge	33	barge	34	sag	35	cage
36	urge	37	shrugs	38	dodge	39	gobs	40	gorge
41	gaze	42	gist	43	gift	44	gems	45	globe

Instructor Notes:	# Correct		

+ = correct   sc = self correct   ⊕ = needed help   ♣   Students in groups only mark words they read.

↑CCCVCC ♣ All Expectancies!

1	cranes	2	waves	3	shacks	4	chops	5	patch	
6	stray	7	muse	8	strikes	9	toads	10	quack	
11	plight	12	since	13	chips	14	fetch	15	bays	
16	pills	17	fence	18	fuse	19	dots	20	chirps	
21	catch	22	pranks	23	batch	24	strain	25	hitch	
26	stance	27	shakes	28	coke	29	quick	30	mute	
31	stretch	32	hoist	33	mills	34	use	35	hence	
36	ditch	37	cobs	38	locks	39	ace	40	dance	
41	shops	42	yuck	43	trench	44	flaunt	45	rails	
46	shrills	47	itch	48	house	49	south	50	strive	
51	wise	52	lay	53	face	54	Nick	55	voles	
56	dense	57	same	58	pain	59	drench	60	docks	
61	match	62	sense	63	fair	64	chance	65	haunt	
66	yaks	67	latch	68	pals	69	teams	70	witch	
71	cons	72	dens	73	streams	74	seems	75	seams	
76	zits	77	strength	78	moles	79	wane	80	stitch	
81	caves	82	sharks	83	strays	84	quince	85	counts	
86	hoist	87	wines	88	coils	89	wrung	90	plain	
91	yeasts	92	dawns	93	maids	94	jousts	95	trades	
96	swirls	97	quilts	98	strung	99	flail	100	pounds	
101	straw	102	straps	103	strains	104	strobe	105	strict	
106	burped	107	matched	108	lugged	109	rigged	110	itched	

Instructor Notes:	# Correct			

+ = correct   sc = self correct   ⊕ = needed help   ♣   Students in groups only mark words they read.

♣ High Frequency Words: 1st 100 words from the Fry List

1	the	2	of	3	and	4	a	5	to	
6	in	7	is	8	you	9	that	10	it	
11	he	12	was	13	for	14	on	15	are	
16	as	17	with	18	his	19	they	20	I	
21	at	22	be	23	this	24	have	25	from	
26	or	27	one	28	had	29	by	30	word	
31	but	32	not	33	what	34	all	35	were	
36	we	37	when	38	your	39	can	40	said	
41	there	42	use	43	an	44	each	45	which	
46	she	47	do	48	how	49	their	50	if	
51	will	52	up	53	other	54	about	55	out	
56	many	57	then	58	them	59	these	60	so	
61	some	62	her	63	would	64	make	65	like	
66	him	67	into	68	time	69	has	70	look	
71	two	72	more	73	write	74	go	75	see	
76	number	77	no	78	way	79	could	80	people	
81	my	82	than	83	first	84	water	85	been	
86	call	87	who	88	am	89	now	90	find	
91	long	92	down	93	day	94	did	95	get	
96	come	97	made	98	may	99	part	100	over	

Instructor Notes:

+ = correct   sc = self correct   ⊕ = needed help   ♣   Students in groups only mark words they read.

♣ High Frequency Words: 2nd 100 words from the Fry List

1	new		2	sound		3	take		4	only		5	little	
6	work		7	know		8	place		9	year		10	live	
11	me		12	back		13	give		14	most		15	very	
16	after		17	thing		18	our		19	just		20	name	
21	good		22	sentence		23	man		24	think		25	say	
26	great		27	where		28	help		29	through		30	much	
31	before		32	line		33	right		34	too		35	mean	
36	old		37	any		38	same		39	tell		40	boy	
41	follow		42	came		43	want		44	show		45	also	
46	around		47	form		48	three		49	small		50	set	
51	put		52	end		53	does		54	another		55	well	
56	large		57	must		58	big		59	even		60	such	
61	because		62	turn		63	here		64	why		65	ask	
66	went		67	men		68	read		69	need		70	land	
71	different		72	home		73	us		74	move		75	try	
76	kind		77	hand		78	picture		79	again		80	change	
81	off		82	play		83	spell		84	air		85	away	
86	animal		87	house		88	point		89	page		90	letter	
91	mother		92	answer		93	found		94	study		95	still	
96	learn		97	should		98	America		99	world		100	high	

Instructor Notes:

+ = correct   sc = self correct   ⊕ = needed help   ♣   Students in groups only mark words they read.

Reading Practice ❖ Sentences with Sight Words

1. I see a red boat.	2. Take the cat to the yard.	3. He was in the car.
4. There is a rat on the ledge!	5. Will you go to the park?	6. This is all I have.
7. Many people are there.	8. Well, well, well, you won!	9. There is a rat in the car!
10. Some people take a bus.	11. This is what I need.	12. He will not take the pen.
13. He was in the big car.	14. Some people drive a car.	15. Call him back to the car!
16. Do you know his name?	17. Will you go to the play?	18. I see a blue boat.
19. First, tell me your name.	20. It is time to write!	21. What time is it now?
22. One day, we will go.	23. Take the cat to the car.	24. First, tell me his name.
25. I see a black boat.	26. Many rats are sick.	27. He was in the fast car.
28. Their house is green.	29. Some people take a plane.	30. Which house is red?
31. Look! The rat is back!	32. I want more food!	33. Do you know her name?
34. You can find it here.	35. Their house is very old.	36. I see a big boat.
37. Take the cat to the house.	38. You did such a good job.	39. You can find it there.
40. Go through the park.	41. I will take three cakes.	42. That is a long train!
43. Will you eat that?	44. Go through the dark.	45. I want more nuts!
46. The rock is very small.	47. He will not take the pill.	48. Their house is very nice.
49. I want more water now!	50. Why did you go there?	51. I see a green boat.
52. He was in the black car.	53. Will you go to the farm?	54. Will we go to that place?
55. Move your picture.	56. I will take three snakes.	57. Tell me that, again.
58. That is what he said.	59. That is a huge train!	60. Take the cat to the vet.
61. That is a big number.	62. We should not move.	63. Ask me to tell you.
64. Stay on this page. ☺	65. Some people write fast.	66. Just think about that!
67. We should not go there.	68. He was in the old car.	69. This is what I will take.
70. Will you go to the moon?	71. I will write a letter.	72. We live in America.

Instructor Notes:

Reading Practice ❖ Sentences with Sight Words

1. He is so little and cute!	2. Now, we will work hard.	3. In one year, I will tell you.
4. He will live, but he is sick.	5. I have a live rat in my car.	6. I have new tools.
7. Say, have you seen a slug?	8. Look at me! I am smart!	9. Give me those socks.
10. Look at me! I am cute!	11. She is a little goof! ☺	12. After lunch, go home.
13. I have new toy cars.	14. Look at me! I am sharp!	15. Help me through it.
16. I hate that, too!	17. He has the right flight.	18. What will he say now?
19. Help! There is a fire!	20. What sound is that?!	21. Our letter is good.
22. Does a ram jam?	23. Does a goat float?	24. Most days, I am here.
25. Take the large plate.	26. Here is the sentence.	27. We are great with words.
28. The men chose the pen.	29. Put that in the sentence.	30. Stay in line, or go back.
31. Most days, I am there.	32. Give me those pens.	33. Only take your coat.
34. After work, go home.	35. The show will start now.	36. I know what you mean.
37. It is now your turn.	38. I do not have much.	39. Quick! Take that out!
40. Does a slug shrug?	41. I have new boots.	42. Most days, I sing.
43. Take your turn now.	44. He has the night flight.	45. I sell good nuts.
46. What will he say next?	47. I will go there, too.	48. Just tell me your name.
49. Even now, I like to sing.	50. Tell them to stay in line.	51. The plane lands on time.
52. Just take the pans.	53. Because, I said so! ☺	54. I have a new cat.
55. You are kind to me.	56. Give us the good food!	57. She is kind to him.
58. Tell them to sing loud!	59. We, too, have strong feet.	60. The show will start soon.
61. Spell the word, "Grinch."	62. The bird is in the air.	63. Take the large barge.
64. Read this page now! ☺	65. Move the toys.	66. Even now, I hate to sing.
67. Spell the word, "Grouch."	68. Our letter needs work.	69. Point to the big bridge.
70. We learn very fast.	71. Read a book to find out!	72. We are cold and old.

Instructor Notes:

Reading Practice ✤ More Sentences!

1. One day last year, I found a rat. He was big, smart and fat. I took him home to keep.

2. The best part of the meal is the fish. I eat the fish first. Then, I ask for cheese and nuts.

3. There is no way I will go to the play. I will skip this time. I need to work at the house.

4. He made a tent in the yard. It was made out of sticks and leaves. It was fun to play in it.

5. Gus drove the old bus. He drove it all over town. People liked Gus and his bus.

6. Would you care to sing me a song? I do not like to sing, but I like to hear people sing.

7. The ship was in the fog. The ship is big. Will the ship hit the rig? I hope not!

8. Chat with me. How will you get to the bus? Will you go through the park?

9. Let us go to the lake. Let us swim in the water. I am hot and need to cool off.

10. The cute cat ate a date. The cat did not like the date. Do you like dates? I do!

11. Pete rode his bike to the park. Pete fell into a hole! But, Pete did not get hurt.

12. We need to stretch our arms now. Or, they will get tight and start to hurt.

13. One day last spring, I was sick. I did not like that! I slept all day and then felt good.

14. Keep that food in the fridge. Or, it could spoil. If it spoils, it could make us sick!

15. Matt fell from the short cliff. He bled from the cuts. Jim drove him home to get help.

16. Let us write down in the letter how we feel. Then, people can read our letter.

17. Your mother has many animals. I like the snake. Can I take a picture of the snake?

18. Would you like to make a cake with me? We can make the cake now. Yum! Yum!

19. I feed my dogs green beans. They like the green beans! They eat them fast.

20. We live in America. It is a big place to live. There are many people who live here.

21. The animal snuck in the house. No one saw the animal. It found a place to sleep.

22. Look at that picture. It has you and me in it. We look cute and sharp in our coats.

23. I need your help. Please help me through the water. I do not know how to swim.

24. What is all the noise?! I need to work. Please stop the noise, so I can get back to work.

Instructor Notes:

Spelling Practice ❖ Regular Words and Sight Words

1.	1.	1.
2.	2.	2.
3.	3.	3.
4.	4.	4.
5.	5.	5.
6.	6.	6.
7.	7.	7.
8.	8.	8.
9.	9.	9.
10.	10.	10.

1.	1.	1.
2.	2.	2.
3.	3.	3.
4.	4.	4.
5.	5.	5.
6.	6.	6.
7.	7.	7.
8.	8.	8.
9.	9.	9.
10.	10.	10.

Instructor Notes:

Spelling Practice ✤ Regular Words and Sight Words

1.	1.	1.
2.	2.	2.
3.	3.	3.
4.	4.	4.
5.	5.	5.
6.	6.	6.
7.	7.	7.
8.	8.	8.
9.	9.	9.
10.	10.	10.

1.	1.	1.
2.	2.	2.
3.	3.	3.
4.	4.	4.
5.	5.	5.
6.	6.	6.
7.	7.	7.
8.	8.	8.
9.	9.	9.
10.	10.	10.

Instructor Notes:

Resources

Books with Practical Instructional Techniques

Archer, A.L. & Hughs, C.A. (2011). Explicit instruction: Effective and efficient teaching. New York, NY: The Guilford Press.

Beck, I.L. (2006). Making sense of phonics: The hows and whys. New York, NY: The Guilford Press.

Beck, I.L. & McKeown, M.G (2006). Improving comprehension with questioning the author. New York: Scholastic.

Bell, N. (2001). Seeing stars. San Luis Obispo, CA: Gander Publishing.

Bell, N. (2007). Visualizing and verbalizing. San Luis Obispo, CA: Gander Publishing.

Brookhart, S.M. (2008). How to give effective feedback to your students. Alexandria, VA: Association for Supervision and Curriculum Development.

Francis, D.J., Rivera, M., Lesaux, N., Kieffer, M., & Rivera, H. (2006). Practical guidelines for the education of English language learners: Research-based recommendations for instruction and academic interventions. Portsmouth, NH: RMC Research Corporation, Center on Instruction.

Fry, E.B. & Kress, J.E. (2006). The reading teacher's book of lists. San Francisco, CA: Jossey-Bass.

Haager, D., Klingner, J. and Vaughn, S. (2007). Evidence-based reading practices for response to intervention. Baltimore, MD: Brookes Publishing Company.

Heacox, D. (2009). Making differentiation a habit: How to ensure success in academically diverse classrooms. Minneapolis, MN: Free Spirit Publishing.

Honig, B., Diamond, L. & Gutlohn, L. (2008). Teaching reading sourcebook. Novato, CA: Arena Press & Berkeley, CA: Consortium on Reading Excellence, Inc. **This is an exceptional resource.**

Linan-Thompson, S. & Vaughn, S. (2007). Research-based methods of reading instruction for English language learners. Alexandria, VA: Association for Supervision and Curriculum Development.

Lindamood, P. & Lindamood, P. (1998). The lindamood phoneme sequencing program (LiPS). Austin, TX: Pro-Ed.

Marzano, R.J. (2007). The art and science of teaching: A comprehensive framework for effective instruction. Alexandria, VA: Association for Supervision and Curriculum Development.

Marzano, R.J. & Pickering, D.J. (2005). Building academic vocabulary: Teacher's manual. Alexandria, VA: Association for Supervision and Curriculum Development.

McCardle, P., Chhabra, V. and Kapinus, B. (2008). Reading research in action: A teacher's guide for student success. Baltimore, MD: Brookes Publishing Company.

Moats, L. C. (2000). Speech to print: Language essentials for teachers. Baltimore, MD: Brookes Publishing Company.

Peery, A., Wiggs, M.D., Piercy, T.D., Lassiter, C.J. & Cebelak, L. (2011). Navigating the English language arts common core state standards. Englewood, CO: Lead and Learn Press.

Reed, D.K., Wexler, J. & Vaughn, S. (2012). RtI for reading at the secondary level: Recommended literacy practices and remaining questions. New York, NY: The Guilford Press.

Walpole, S. & McKenna, M.C. (2012). The literacy coach's handbook: Second edition. New York, NY: The Guilford Press.

Books Outlining Research Findings

August, D. and Shanahan, T. (editors) (2008). Developing reading and writing in second-language learners: Lessons from the Report of the National Literacy Panel on language-minority children and youth. Co-published by Routledge, The Center for Applied Linguistics and the International Reading Association.

McCardle, P. and Chhabra, V. (editors) (2004). The voice of evidence. Baltimore, MD: Brookes Publishing Company.

National Institute of Child Health and Human Development. (2000). Report of the National Reading Panel. Teaching children to read: An evidence-based assessment of the scientific research literature on reading and its implications for reading instruction (NIH Publication No. 00-4769). Washington, DC: U.S. Government Printing Office.

Pressley, M., Collins-Block, C. and Gambrell, L. (2002). Improving comprehension instruction: Rethinking research, theory, and classroom practice. Delaware, International Reading Association.

Snow, C.E., Burns, M.S. and Griffin, P. (Eds.). (1998). Preventing reading difficulties in young children. Washington DC: National Academies Press.

Snow, C.E., Burns, M.S. and Griffin, P. (Eds.). (2005). Knowledge to support the teaching of reading. San Francisco, CA: Jossey Bass.

Sousa, David A. (2005). How the brain learns to read. Thousand Oaks, CA: Corwin Press.

Sousa, David A. (2010). How the ELL brain learns. Thousand Oaks, CA: Corwin Press.

Stanovich, P. J., & Stanovich, K. E. (2003). Using research and reason in education: How teachers can use scientifically based research to make curricular & instructional decisions. Washington, DC: US Department of Education.

Torgesen, J.K., Houston, D.D., Rissman, L.M., Decker, S.M., Roberts, G., Vaugn, S., Wexler, J., Francis, D.J., Rivera, M.O., Lesaux, N. (2007). Academic literacy instruction for adolescents: A guidance document from the Center on Instruction. NH: RMC Research. Corporation, Center on Instruction.

Web Sites

✣ABC Mouse: http://www.abcmouse.com/ *Kid's Site

✣Alliance for Excellent Education: http://www.all4ed.org/

✣Center for the Improvement of Early Reading Achievement: www.ciera.org

✣Center on Instruction: http://www.centeroninstruction.org/

✣Doing What Works: http://dww.ed.gov/

✣Ed Helper: http://edhelper.com/

✣Florida Center for Reading Research: www.fcrr.org

✣Fun Brain: http://www.funbrain.com/ *Kid's Site

✣Get Ready To Read: http://www.getreadytoread.org/

✣International Dyslexia Association: www.interdys.org

✣International Reading Association: www.reading.org

✣Kids.Gov: http://www.kids.gov/

✣LD Online: http://www.ldonline.org/

✣Let's Go Learn: http://www.letsgolearn.com/ *Kid's Site

✣Lexia: http://www.lexialearning.com/ *Kid's Site

✣Library of Congress: http://www.loc.gov/index.html *Kid's Site

- ✛Lindamood-Bell: http://www.lindamoodbell.com/
- ✛National Center for Learning Disabilities: www.ncld.org
- ✛National Center on Student Progress Monitoring: www.studentprogress.org
- ✛National Institute for Literacy: http://www.nifl.gov/
- ✛National Reading Panel: www.nationalreadingpanel.org
- ✛PBS Kids: http://pbskids.org/lions/ ***Kid's Site**
- ✛Reading Plus: http://www.readingplus.com/ ***Kid's Site**
- ✛Reading Rockets: www.readingrockets.org
- ✛Star Fall: http://www.starfall.com/ ***Kid's Site**
- ✛SW Educational Development Laboratory (SEDL) Reading Resources: www.sedl.org/reading/rad/
- ✛United States Department of Education: www.ed.gov
- ✛What Works Clearinghouse: http://ies.ed.gov/ncee/wwc/

Web Resources

Building the Foundation: A Suggested Progression of Sub-skills to Achieve the Reading Standards: Foundational Skills in the Common Core State Standards:
http://www.centeroninstruction.org/files/Building%20the%20Foundation.pdf

Carol Ann Tomlinson Article (1995): Differentiating Instruction for Advanced Learners in the Mixed-Ability Middle School Classroom: http://www.curriculumassociates.com/professional-development/topics/DiffInstruction/extras/lesson1/ra1_5.pdf

Common Core State Standards (2010): Developed by the National Governors Association Center for Best Practices, Council of Chief State School Officers: http://www.corestandards.org/

Developing Early Literacy (2008). Report of the National Early Literacy Panel:
http://www.nifl.gov/publications/pdf/NELPReport09.pdf

Double the Work: Challenges and Solutions to Acquiring Language and Academic Literacy for Adolescent English Language Learners (2007): http://www.all4ed.org/files/DoubleWork.pdf

Effective Instruction for Adolescent Struggling Readers (2008):
http://www.centeroninstruction.org/files/Adol%20Struggling%20Readers%20Practice%20Brief.pdf

Improving Literacy Instruction in Middle and High Schools: A Guide for Principals (2007):
http://www.fcrr.org/Interventions/pdf/Principals%20Guide-Secondary.pdf

Literacy Instruction in the Content Areas: Getting to the Core of Middle and High School Improvement:
http://www.all4ed.org/files/LitCon.pdf

National Reading Technical Assistance Center: A Review of the Current Research on Vocabulary Instruction (2010): http://www2.ed.gov/programs/readingfirst/support/rmcfinal1.pdf

President Obama's Blueprint for Reform: http://www2.ed.gov/policy/elsec/leg/blueprint/blueprint.pdf

School Improvement By Design: Lessons From a Study of Comprehensive School Reform Programs (2009). Consortium for Policy Research in Education:
http://www.cpre.org/images/stories/cpre_pdfs/sii%20final%20report_web%20file.pdf

Using Student Achievement Data to Support Instructional Decision Making (2009). USDOE and IES and What Works Clearinghouse: http://ies.ed.gov/ncee/wwc/pdf/practiceguides/dddm_pg_092909.pdf

Writing Next: Effective Strategies to Improve Writing of Adolescents in Middle and High Schools (2007):
http://www.all4ed.org/files/WritingNext.pdf

Disclaimers

Lindamood-Bell Disclaimer: Lindamood-Bell Learning Process®, Lindamood-Bell®, Lindamood®, and Lindamood Phoneme Sequencing® are trademarks of Lindamood-Bell Learning Processes. Lindamood-Bell in no way guarantees the quality of the materials or services that are associated with the publications or services of the American Reading Corps and Mary Spencer. The American Reading Corps and Mary Spencer are not affiliated with, certified, endorsed, licensed, monitored or sponsored by Lindamood-Bell, Nanci Bell, Phyllis Lindamood, or Pat Lindamood.

Final Note: Volume Two of this series will focus on multisyllable words. The anticipated publication date is early 2013.

Do you have suggestions on the improvement of this resource? I would love your feedback. Please email me at americanreadingcorps@gmail.com with your suggestions. Thank you _very_ much.

Mary L. Spencer, M.Ed., Founder, American Reading Corps

American Reading Corps

"Books are the carriers of civilization. Without books, history is silent, literature dumb, science crippled, thought and speculation at a standstill. Without books, the development of civilization would have been impossible. They are engines of change (as Thoreau said), windows on the world and lighthouses erected in the sea of time. They are companions, teachers, magicians, bankers of the treasures of the mind. Books are humanity in print." — **Barbara W. Tuchman**